# MACBOOK SENIORS GUIDE 2025

Practical How-To Manual for First-Time Users to
Explore Every Features, Navigate macOS, and Use
Your Laptop with Confidence and Clarity

## ALBERT F. JOHNSON

# DISCLAIMER

This book is for educational and informational purposes only. It is not affiliated with or endorsed by Apple Inc. All product names and trademarks belong to their respective owners.

While every effort has been made to ensure accuracy, the author and publisher are not responsible for any errors, changes in software, or outcomes resulting from the use of this guide. For the most up-to-date information, please refer to Apple's official support.

Always use your own judgment, and seek professional help if you're unsure about any steps.

# TABLE OF CONTENT

# Introduction

If you're holding this book in your hands —
or opening it on a screen — let me start by
saying: **you're exactly where you need to be.**

Whether this is your very first time using a
MacBook, or you've been trying to figure it
out on your own for a while, this guide is
here to help — patiently, clearly, and without
any pressure. Because learning something
new, especially when it comes to
technology, isn't about how young or fast
you are. It's about having the right support.

## Why This Book Exists

Too many seniors have been made to feel
like they've "missed the boat" when it comes
to technology. Maybe you've asked for help
and felt brushed off. Or maybe every time

you try to learn, the instructions are filled with tech jargon, tiny print, and steps that assume you already know more than you do.

This book was written to change that. It was created to say: **you are not behind. You are not alone. And yes — you absolutely can do this.**

Your MacBook is an incredible tool. But like any new tool, it's easier to use when someone shows you how — with patience, plain English, and a smile.

## What You'll Find Inside

You'll learn how to:

- **Turn on and set up your MacBook** from scratch

- Understand what all the icons, menus, and buttons really do

9

- Use email, FaceTime, Safari, and Photos with ease

- Adjust settings for **larger text**, better sound, and better visibility

- Stay **safe online** and avoid common scams

- Download helpful apps, manage files, and keep your Mac organized

- Troubleshoot small issues *without panic or frustration*

Every chapter includes **step-by-step instructions,** and **simple explanations** that never assume prior knowledge.

You don't need to be "tech-savvy." You don't need to have grown up using computers.

You just need a willingness to learn — and this guide will take care of the rest.

**Take Your Time — This is Your Journey**

This isn't a race. You can take it one chapter at a time, skip around to what you're most curious about, or go through it with a friend or family member.

There's no pressure here — just progress. Small, steady progress that builds real confidence.

Many people pick up this book because they want to feel less afraid of their MacBook. But what they walk away with is so much more: **freedom, connection, and a renewed sense of independence.**

Imagine video calling your grandchildren, organizing your family photos, browsing recipes, watching your favorite shows, or writing your memoirs — all on your own MacBook.

That's not only possible — it's about to become easy.

So let's begin this journey together. **You're capable. You're smart. You're ready.**

And most importantly, you're not alone.

# Chapter 1: Getting Started

## What Is a MacBook and Why It's Different

A **MacBook** is a type of laptop made by Apple. It's small, light, and powerful — meaning you can use it anywhere to do everyday things like browsing the internet, writing emails, watching videos, or talking to loved ones on video calls.

What makes a MacBook different from other laptops is how it looks, how it feels, and how simple it can be once you understand it. Apple designs its products to be clean and user-friendly, but if you're new to it, things might look unfamiliar at first. That's okay — this guide will help you get comfortable, step by step.

There are two main types of MacBooks:

- **MacBook Air** – This is the lighter, thinner model. It's great for everyday use.

- **MacBook Pro** – This is a bit heavier and faster, often used for more demanding tasks like editing photos or videos.

Whichever one you have, this book applies to both. You don't need to worry about the technical details. If it says "MacBook" on the front, you're in the right place.

## Models Overview: Air vs. Pro (and How to Know Yours)

To check which MacBook model you have:

1. Click the **Apple logo** in the top-left corner of your screen.

2. Select **"About This Mac."**

3. A window will appear showing the model (e.g., "MacBook Air (M1, 2020)" or "MacBook Pro (2022)").

Knowing your model can help if you ever need to contact Apple Support or install updates. But for most of this book, you won't need to think about it again — we'll keep things simple and universal.

**Tip:** Write down your model name on a sticky note and keep it inside your book for future reference.

## Charging, Turning On, and Using the Trackpad

Let's get your MacBook up and running.

**How to Charge:**

- Plug the small end of the charging cable into the **port** on the side of your MacBook.

- Plug the other end into a wall outlet.

- A little lightning symbol on the screen will show it's charging.

**Note:** MacBooks use **MagSafe** or **USB-C** chargers depending on the model. Don't worry — both work the same way.

**How to Turn It On:**

- Simply **lift the lid** of your MacBook — it should turn on automatically.

- If it doesn't, press the **power button** (usually in the top-right corner of the keyboard or part of the Touch ID button).

Once it's on, you'll see the Apple logo and then your desktop or login screen.

**Understanding the Trackpad:**

The trackpad is the large, flat square just below the keyboard. It's like a mouse, but built in.

Here's how to use it:

- **Move your finger** on it to move the pointer on the screen.

- **Tap with one finger** to click something.

- **Tap twice quickly** to double-click.

- **Click and hold**, then drag your finger to move items (like dragging a file).

- **Use two fingers** to scroll up or down — just like swiping on a phone.

Take a moment to try it out. It may feel new at first, but most seniors find it easier than using a separate mouse once they get used to it.

## Understanding the Desktop and Basic Navigation

Once your MacBook starts, you'll see the **desktop** — this is your home base, like your desk in the real world.

Here's what you'll notice:

**The Desktop:**

- You might see a **background picture** (wallpaper) and a few **icons** — like your hard drive or downloaded files.

- Think of it like a table where you can place things you want easy access to.

**The Menu Bar (Top of the Screen):**

- On the **left**, you'll see the **Apple logo**. Click it for system settings like shutting down or restarting.

- Next to it are menus that change depending on the program you're using (e.g., "Safari" or "Photos").

- On the **right**, you'll see small symbols — Wi-Fi, battery life, sound, date/time.

**The Dock (Bottom of the Screen):**

- This is a row of **app icons** — it's like a tool tray.

- Click an icon to open a program (e.g., Safari to browse the web).

- You can add or remove apps from the Dock anytime.

**The Finder:**

- The **Finder** is the blue-and-white smiling face icon on the Dock.

- Click it to open your files, photos, and folders. Think of it like your digital file cabinet.

## Quick Practice Exercise

☑ Turn on your MacBook

☑ Move the pointer using the trackpad

☑ Click the Finder icon in the Dock

☑ Open a folder (like "Downloads")

☑ Close the window by clicking the red circle at the top-left

If you just did that, congrats! You're already navigating your MacBook like a pro.

# Chapter 2: Mastering the Keyboard and Trackpad

## Keyboard Basics and Special Keys

Your MacBook keyboard is your main way of typing letters, numbers, and commands. While it looks like any standard keyboard, Apple includes a few extra keys that may be unfamiliar if you're new to Macs.

Let's break it down:

**Most Common Keys:**

- **Letters (A–Z)** and **Numbers (0–9)** — same as any keyboard.

- **Spacebar** – adds a space between words.

- **Return/Enter** – starts a new line or confirms an action.

- **Delete** – erases the character to the left of the cursor.

**Special Mac Keys:**

- **Command (⌘)** – Often used with other keys (e.g., Command + C to copy).

- **Option (⌥)** – Adds extra functions when pressed with other keys.

- **Control (Ctrl)** – Used for certain shortcuts.

- **Function (fn)** – Found in the bottom left; can be used to access special functions or dictate text (newer models).

- **Escape (esc)** – Cancels actions or closes small windows.

- **Touch ID (on newer models)** – Acts like a fingerprint button for unlocking your Mac.

**Tip for Seniors:** If you're not sure what a key does, try pressing it gently and watching what happens — nothing harmful will occur. Most functions can be undone.

## How to Use the Trackpad Gestures

The **trackpad** is Apple's version of a mouse — it responds to finger movements, called **gestures**. Here are the most helpful ones to know as a beginner:

Basic Gestures:

- **One-finger move:** Slide one finger across the trackpad to move the cursor.

- **One-finger tap:** Select or click on something (like a button or file).

- **Double-tap:** Opens items, like double-clicking with a mouse.

- **Click and drag:** Press down on the trackpad and move your finger to drag a window or file.

Helpful Two-Finger Gestures:

- **Scroll up/down:** Place two fingers on the trackpad and slide up or down to scroll through pages.

- **Right-click:** Tap with two fingers at once. A small menu will appear — this is like a "right click" on a traditional mouse.

- **Zoom (optional):** Pinch two fingers together or apart (just like on a smartphone) to zoom in or out on some apps.

🧠 **Practice Tip:** Try opening Safari (the web browser), place two fingers on the trackpad, and scroll up and down through a website. That motion will become second nature over time.

## Adjusting Keyboard Size and Mouse Speed for Comfort

Comfort matters — especially when using your MacBook for longer periods. Apple gives you easy ways to adjust your keyboard and trackpad so they feel better for your hands and eyes.

**Make Keyboard Text Larger:**

This doesn't change the keyboard itself, but it helps make the words on your screen easier to see when you type.

1. Click the **Apple logo** (top-left corner).

2. Choose **System Settings** (or "System Preferences" on older Macs).

3. Go to **Display**.

4. Use the **Text Size** slider to make things bigger.

**Adjust Trackpad Speed:**

If the pointer moves too fast or too slow, you can fix that.

1. Go to **System Settings**.

2. Click **Trackpad**.

3. Find the **Tracking Speed** slider — move it left for slower, right for faster.

**Change Key Repeat or Delay:**

If you find letters repeating too quickly while typing, do this:

1. In **System Settings**, go to **Keyboard**.

2. Adjust the **Key Repeat** and **Delay Until Repeat** sliders to slower speeds.

**Turn on Touch ID (optional):**

Newer MacBooks allow you to unlock your Mac with your fingerprint.

1. Go to **System Settings**.

2. Click **Touch ID & Password**.

3. Follow the instructions to add your fingerprint.

This can save you from having to type your password every time!

## Quick Recap

☑ You learned the main keys on your keyboard and what they do

☑ You practiced basic and two-finger gestures on the trackpad

☑ You found out how to make text bigger and the cursor easier to control

☑ You're getting more comfortable with your Mac already!

Take your time. If something didn't click the first time, go back and try again. The more you practice, the more natural it will feel — and you're doing just fine.

# Chapter 3: macOS Made Simple

## What Is macOS? (A Beginner's Tour)

When you open your MacBook, the system that makes everything run — from clicking on icons to browsing the internet — is called **macOS**. It's the **Mac operating system**, and you can think of it like the brain behind your computer.

Every few years, Apple updates macOS to make things faster, safer, and more useful. The most recent version at the time of this writing is called **macOS Sonoma**, but whether you're using Sonoma or an earlier version like Ventura or Monterey, the basics in this guide will still apply.

macOS is designed to be clean and simple, but it can feel unfamiliar if you're used to Windows or haven't used a computer in a long time. That's why this chapter focuses on helping you feel at home.

## Sonoma and Beyond: What's New

If your MacBook is running **macOS Sonoma**, here are a few new features you might notice:

- **Widgets on your desktop** – Small tools like clocks, weather, or reminders you can add to your main screen.

- **New screen savers** – Scenic videos that appear when your Mac is idle.

- **Better video call tools** – More fun and useful features for FaceTime and Zoom.

- **Stronger privacy tools** – Better protection while browsing online.

Don't worry — you don't need to learn everything all at once. This book will show you how to use the features that matter most.

To check your version:

1. Click the **Apple logo** in the top-left corner.

2. Select **About This Mac.**

3. The version of macOS you're using will appear near the top.

## Finding and Opening Apps with the Dock and Launchpad

macOS includes many useful **apps** (short for "applications") — like Safari for internet, Mail for email, and Photos for your pictures. There are two easy ways to open them:

## 1. The Dock (Bottom of Your Screen)

- The Dock is the row of icons at the bottom of your screen. It's like your shortcut bar.

- Click any icon in the Dock to open that app.

- You can move icons around or remove ones you don't use by dragging them off the Dock.

## Common Dock Icons You'll See:

- **Finder (smiley face)** – Opens your files

- **Safari (compass)** – Internet browser

- **Mail (envelope)** – Email

- **Messages (speech bubble)** – Texting

- **Photos (flower)** – Your pictures

To add an app to the Dock:

- Open the app from **Launchpad** or **Finder** (see below), then **right-click** its icon in the Dock and choose *"Keep in Dock."*

## 2. Launchpad (Grid of Apps)

- Click the **Launchpad icon** (looks like a silver rocket) in the Dock.

- All your apps will appear in a grid, like a smartphone screen.

- Click on any app to open it.

  **Tip:** If Launchpad has too many icons, type the app name in the search bar at the top.

# Managing Windows, Menus, and the Finder

When you open apps, they appear in **windows** — boxes you can move, shrink, or close. Let's explore how to manage them:

### The Red, Yellow, Green Buttons:

At the top-left of every window, you'll see three small circles:

- **Red** closes the window.

- **Yellow** minimizes (hides) the window in the Dock.

- **Green** makes the window full-screen or exits full-screen.

### Moving and Resizing Windows:

- Click and **drag the top bar** of a window to move it.

34

- Move your pointer to the edges or corners to **resize** the window.

**The Menu Bar:**

Located at the very **top of your screen**, this bar changes depending on what app you're using.

For example, if you're in Safari, you'll see "Safari" menus with words like "File," "Edit," and "View." Click each word to explore options — like printing, saving, or undoing actions.

**Using Finder to Organize Your Mac:**

The **Finder** is your file manager — think of it like your digital filing cabinet.

To open it:

1. Click the **Finder icon** (the blue and white smiley face) in the Dock.

2. You'll see folders on the left, such as:

- ○ **Documents**

- ○ **Downloads**

- ○ **Desktop**

- ○ **Applications**

You can open these folders to find files, organize them into new folders, or delete anything you no longer need.

To create a new folder:

- Right-click anywhere in the Finder window and choose **New Folder**.

- Type a name and press **Return**.

## Quick Recap

☑ You now know what **macOS** is and what it does

☑ You learned the difference between the **Dock** and **Launchpad**

☑ You explored how to **move, resize, and close windows**

☑ You got familiar with the **Finder** — your digital file cabinet

Remember: no need to memorize everything. The more you explore, the more familiar it will feel. And every time you try something new, you're learning.

# Chapter 4: Personalizing Your MacBook

One of the best things about your MacBook is how easily you can make it **feel like your own**. From making the text larger to changing your background photo, personalizing your MacBook helps it become easier to use — and more enjoyable, too.

## Changing Wallpaper and Display Settings

Your **wallpaper** is the background image you see on your desktop. Apple gives you many beautiful choices, but you can also use a personal photo if you'd like.

To **Change Your Wallpaper:**

1. Click the **Apple logo** at the top-left corner of your screen.

2. Select **System Settings** (or *System Preferences*).

3. Choose **Wallpaper** or **Desktop & Screen Saver**.

4. Browse through the available images and click one to select it.

If you want to use your own photo:

- Click **Photos** from the side menu.

- Select an image from your albums.

**Tip:** Choose something calming or meaningful — like a family picture or scenic view — to make your desktop feel more inviting.

**Adjusting Display Brightness:**

- Go to **System Settings** > **Displays**.

- Use the **Brightness slider** to make the screen lighter or darker.

A brighter screen is good during the day, but a slightly dimmer one can feel more comfortable in the evening.

## Enlarging Text and Icons for Better Visibility

If you find the text too small, don't worry — your MacBook has built-in options to **make everything easier to see**.

To Increase Text Size:

1. Go to **System Settings** > **Displays**.

2. Under **Text Size**, slide the bar to the right to enlarge the system text.

This will make menu bar text, buttons, and app names bigger.

To Increase Icon Size (for folders/files):

1. Open any folder using **Finder**.

2. Right-click anywhere in the blank space and choose **Show View Options**.

3. Adjust the **Icon Size** and **Text Size** sliders.

You can also move icons around by clicking and dragging them — organize things however makes sense to you.

## Setting Up Night Shift, Dark Mode, and Zoom

These features help reduce eye strain, especially in low light or during long computer sessions.

**Night Shift:**

This feature makes your screen warmer (less blue) in the evening, which is gentler on your eyes.

To turn it on:

1. Go to **System Settings** > **Displays** > **Night Shift**.

2. Choose to have it turn on **Automatically** from sunset to sunrise.

**Dark Mode:**

Dark Mode switches your screen to darker colors. Many seniors find this easier to read, especially at night.

To enable:

1. Go to **System Settings** > **Appearance**.

2. Choose **Dark**.

You can switch back to **Light** mode anytime.

Zoom (Screen Magnifier):

Zoom lets you **enlarge any part of the screen**, which is helpful for reading small text.

To turn it on:

1. Go to **System Settings** > **Accessibility** > **Zoom**.

2. Toggle the switch **on**.

Once enabled, you can press and hold **Control (^)** and scroll with two fingers to zoom in or out.

## Adjusting Sound, Volume, and Notifications

Let's make sure your MacBook sounds and alerts work the way you want them to — no sudden loud noises or missed messages.

**To Adjust Volume:**

- Use the **volume keys** on the top row of your keyboard.

- Or go to **System Settings** > **Sound** to adjust the volume manually.

You can also:

- Choose your **alert sound**

- Adjust **output devices** (like headphones or speakers)

- Enable **mute** if you want complete silence

**Managing Notifications:**

Notifications are small pop-up messages that tell you when something happens — like a new email or calendar reminder.

To manage them:

1. Go to **System Settings** > **Notifications**.

2. Select an app (like Mail or Messages).

3. Choose whether it shows alerts, sounds, or nothing at all.

Tip: If your Mac feels too "noisy" with alerts, it's perfectly fine to turn off notifications for apps you don't use often.

## Quick Recap

☑ You changed your wallpaper and screen brightness

☑ You made text and icons larger for better visibility

☑ You learned how to use **Night Shift**, **Dark Mode**, and **Zoom**

☑ You adjusted sound and notifications for a calmer experience

The more you personalize your MacBook, the more natural and comfortable it will feel

— just like adjusting a pair of reading glasses until everything's perfectly clear.

# Chapter 5: Staying Connected

Your MacBook isn't just a tool — it's your window to the world. Whether you're emailing a loved one, browsing your favorite websites, or printing out a recipe, **being connected** is what makes everything work smoothly.

This chapter walks you through how to connect to Wi-Fi, pair Bluetooth devices, and use printers or USB drives — all without the tech stress

## Setting Up Wi-Fi and Bluetooth

### How to Connect to Wi-Fi:

Wi-Fi gives your MacBook access to the internet, so you can browse, email, video chat, and more.

1. Look at the **top-right corner** of your screen.

2. Click the **Wi-Fi symbol** (it looks like a fan or radio waves).

3. A list of available networks will appear.

4. Click the one that matches your home network name.

5. Enter the **Wi-Fi password** (this is usually printed on the back of your modem or router).

6. Click **Join**.

Once you're connected, your Mac will remember your network — no need to enter the password again next time.

**Tip:** If you travel or visit friends, you can connect to their Wi-Fi in the same way.

# How to Turn On Bluetooth:

Bluetooth allows your Mac to wirelessly connect with other devices like headphones, keyboards, and speakers.

1. Click the **Apple logo** in the top-left.

2. Go to **System Settings** > **Bluetooth**.

3. Toggle Bluetooth **ON** (if it's not already).

4. Your Mac will search for nearby devices.

5. When you see your device (e.g., "JBL Speaker" or "Logitech Mouse"), click **Connect**.

Most devices will pair in seconds. If prompted, follow any extra instructions shown on screen.

🐝 **Bluetooth Tip for Seniors:** Wireless headphones are great if you want to listen to music or watch videos without disturbing anyone — and once paired, your Mac will connect automatically the next time.

## Connecting Printers and External Devices

Sometimes, you'll want to **print a document**, **view photos from a flash drive**, or **connect an external keyboard**. Your MacBook makes it easy — even if it's your first time.

**To Connect a Printer (Wired or Wireless):**

1. Plug the printer into your MacBook via USB **or** connect it to the same Wi-Fi network.

2. Open **System Settings** > **Printers & Scanners**.

3. Click the **Add Printer** button.

4. Your Mac will detect the printer. Click it, then click **Add**.

You can now print from any app — like Safari, Mail, or Notes — by going to **File > Print**, or pressing **Command + P**.

**To Use a USB Drive:**

1. Plug the USB drive into a port on your MacBook. (If your Mac has only USB-C ports, use a small adapter.)

2. The drive will appear on your **desktop** or in **Finder** under *Locations*.

3. Click to open, view, copy, or move files.

**Tip:** Always **eject the drive safely** before unplugging. Right-click on the USB icon and select **Eject**, or drag it to the trash bin (which turns into an Eject icon).

## Connecting External Accessories:

Want to plug in a **keyboard, mouse, external hard drive**, or **SD card reader**?

- For wired devices: Plug directly into the MacBook or a USB adapter.

- For wireless devices: Use **Bluetooth** (covered above).

## Common Troubleshooting Tips:

- If your Mac doesn't recognize a device, try unplugging and plugging it back in.

- Restarting the Mac often solves connection problems.

- Make sure the device is powered on or charged.

## Quick Recap

☑ You connected to Wi-Fi — your link to the internet

☑ You turned on Bluetooth and paired wireless accessories

☑ You set up a printer and learned how to use USB drives

☑ You gained confidence using external devices with ease

Being connected is more than a tech feature — it's your bridge to communication, learning, entertainment, and joy. And now that you know how to stay connected, the digital world is right at your fingertips.

# Chapter 6: Internet and Email Essentials

Once you're connected to Wi-Fi, the **internet** becomes your gateway to the world — whether you're searching for information, reading the news, or chatting with loved ones. This chapter helps you get comfortable using **Safari** (Apple's web browser) and **Mail** (your email app), two essential tools for daily life on your MacBook.

## Using Safari: Browsing the Web Safely

**Safari** is the app that lets you explore websites. It's represented by a blue compass icon — you'll find it on your **Dock** at the bottom of the screen.

How to Open Safari:

- Click the **Safari icon** once to open it.

- The main window will open with a search bar at the top.

**To Visit a Website:**

1. Click inside the **address bar** at the top.

2. Type a website name (like *www.bbc.com* or *www.google.com*).

3. Press **Return** on your keyboard.

Or simply type a question or topic — Safari will search the internet for you!

**Tips for Safe Browsing:**

- Look for websites that start with **https** — the "s" stands for secure.

- Avoid clicking pop-ups or ads that seem suspicious.

- Never enter personal info on a site unless you trust it.

🔖 **Safari Shortcut:** To go back to a previous page, click the **left arrow** at the top-left of the Safari window.

## Creating and Managing Bookmarks

If you visit certain websites often — like news, recipes, or your bank — you can **save them as bookmarks** so you don't have to type the address every time.

**To Add a Bookmark:**

1. While on the website, click **"Bookmarks"** in the menu bar at the top.

2. Choose **Add Bookmark.**

56

3. Name it something easy to remember and click **Add**.

To open a saved bookmark:

- Click **Bookmarks** in the top menu again and select the one you saved.

You can also organize bookmarks into folders if you have several you want to keep handy.

## Setting Up and Using Apple Mail

Apple's built-in **Mail app** makes it easy to send and receive emails. The icon looks like a postage stamp — click it in your Dock to get started.

**To Set Up Email:**

1. Open **Mail** for the first time.

2. It will ask you to sign in with your **email address and password**.

3. Follow the instructions — your email will be added to the app.

Mail works with Gmail, Yahoo, iCloud, Outlook, and most other email services.

**To Read Your Email:**

- Open the **Mail app**.

- On the left, you'll see your **Inbox**. Click to view new messages.

- Click a message to read it in full on the right side.

**To Write a New Email:**

1. Click the **New Message** icon (a square with a pencil).

2. Enter the person's email address in the "To" field.

3. Add a **Subject** — like "Hello!" or "Family Photos."

4. Type your message.

5. Click **Send** (paper airplane icon).

   **Tip:** You can also attach photos by clicking the **paperclip icon** in the message window and selecting files from your Mac.

## Avoiding Spam and Phishing Emails

While most emails are safe, some may try to trick you into giving away personal information. These are called **spam** or **phishing emails**.

**Signs of a Suspicious Email:**

- It says you won a prize you didn't enter.

- It asks you to confirm your bank details or password.

- It has lots of spelling errors or feels urgent.

If something looks odd, do **not** click any links or reply.

To delete it:

- Select the message and click the **Trash** icon.

To report it as junk:

- Click the **Junk** button in the Mail toolbar.

☑ Remember: Your bank or Apple will never ask for sensitive info by email.

## Quick Recap

☑ You learned how to use **Safari** to browse the internet safely

☑ You saved your favorite websites using **Bookmarks**

☑ You set up and used the **Mail app** to send and receive emails

☑ You learned how to recognize and avoid **email scams**

The internet can be a wonderful place when used wisely — and now, you've taken a huge step toward using it with confidence and care.

# Chapter 7: Communicating with Family and Friends

One of the greatest joys of owning a MacBook is being able to **stay close to the people you care about**, no matter how far apart you may be. Whether it's a video call with your grandchildren or sending a quick "thinking of you" message to a friend, your Mac makes it easy — and enjoyable.

## Setting Up FaceTime and Video Calls

**FaceTime** is Apple's built-in app for video and audio calls. It's free to use and works on any Apple device — including iPhones, iPads, and MacBooks.

**To Open FaceTime:**

- Click the **FaceTime icon** (a green video camera) in your Dock or Launchpad.

**To Set It Up:**

1. Sign in with your **Apple ID** (the same one you use for the App Store or iCloud).

2. Make sure your **camera and microphone** are turned on (they usually turn on automatically).

**To Make a FaceTime Call:**

1. Open the FaceTime app.

2. In the search bar at the top, type the name, phone number, or email address of the person you want to call.

3. Click **Video** to start a video call, or **Audio** for a voice-only call.

**Tip:** If the person is saved in your Contacts, just start typing their name, and it will pop up.

**During the Call:**

- Click the **red button** to hang up.

- Click the **camera** or **mute** icons to turn video or sound on/off.

**Helpful Tip for Seniors:** FaceTime is private, safe, and perfect for "seeing" your loved ones when a visit isn't possible — especially during holidays or special moments.

## Using Messages to Stay in Touch

**Messages** lets you send text messages, photos, links, and even emojis — just like on a smartphone. It's fast, easy, and built into your MacBook.

64

## To Open Messages:

- Click the **Messages icon** (a blue speech bubble) in your Dock.

## To Send a Message:

1. Click the **New Message** icon (square with a pencil).

2. Enter the person's phone number, Apple ID email, or select from your Contacts.

3. Type your message in the box at the bottom.

4. Press **Return** to send it.

## To Add a Photo:

- Click the **Photos icon** next to the text box.

- Choose a photo from your library.

**To Use Emojis:**

- Click the **smiley face icon** to add fun expressions to your message.

Messages work between all Apple devices — so if your family uses iPhones or iPads, they'll receive your texts instantly.

**Bonus Tip:** You can also send group messages to multiple people at once — perfect for keeping the whole family in the loop.

## Sharing Photos and Files via iCloud

**iCloud** is Apple's secure storage system that lets you share photos, files, and documents across all your Apple devices — or even with others by email or link.

**To Use iCloud for Photos:**

66

1. Click the **Photos app** (a colorful flower icon).

2. Make sure **iCloud Photos** is turned on by going to:

   ○ **System Settings > Apple ID > iCloud > Photos** → Turn it **ON**.

3. Any photo added to your Mac will now be available on your iPhone, iPad, or other Apple devices (and vice versa).

**To Share a Photo with Someone:**

1. Open **Photos** and select the picture.

2. Click the **Share button** (a square with an arrow pointing up).

3. Choose **Mail** or **Messages**, depending on how you want to send it.

**To Share a File from Finder:**

1. Open **Finder** and locate the file.

2. Right-click the file and choose **Share** > **Mail**, **Messages**, or **Copy Link** (if using iCloud Drive).

iCloud also keeps your important documents safe — even if something happens to your computer.

## Quick Recap

☑ You learned how to use **FaceTime** for video and audio calls

☑ You sent messages using the **Messages app**

☑ You shared photos and documents safely through **iCloud**

With just a few clicks, you can stay connected — not just through words, but through smiles, stories, and shared moments. Your MacBook isn't just a machine; it's your bridge to the people who matter most.

# Chapter 8: Managing Files and Folders

Your MacBook isn't just a tool for emails and browsing — it's a place where you can **store and organize everything important to you:** documents, family photos, letters, recipes, and more. In this chapter, we'll walk through how to create, save, find, and organize files and folders with confidence.

## Creating, Saving, and Organizing Files

When you use an app like **Pages** (for writing) or **Preview** (for reading documents), you can **save your work as a file** and store it on your Mac for future use.

### Creating and Saving a File:

Let's say you write a letter using **Pages:**

1. Open the **Pages** app.

2. Type your letter.

3. When you're done, click **File** in the top-left menu bar.

4. Choose **Save** or **Save As**.

5. Give your file a name — for example, *"Letter to Sarah."*

6. Choose where to save it (we suggest the **Documents** folder).

7. Click **Save.**

Your file is now saved — and can be opened, edited, or shared any time.

**Organizing Files into Folders:**

To keep things tidy, it's a good idea to put related files into folders — just like you would in a filing cabinet.

1. Open the **Finder** (smiley face icon in the Dock).

2. Navigate to the folder where you want to create a new one (like Documents).

3. Right-click anywhere in the white space.

4. Click **New Folder.**

5. Give it a name (like "Family Letters" or "Recipes") and press **Return.**

6. Now, you can **drag files into the folder** to stay organized.

**Tip:** If you ever lose track of where you saved something, don't worry — we'll cover that next.

## Using Finder to Locate Anything

**Finder** is your Mac's built-in tool for finding and organizing files — think of it like your personal assistant for everything on your computer.

**To Open Finder:**

- Click the **Finder icon** (smiling face) on your Dock.

The Finder window has two parts:

- **Sidebar on the left:** Quick access to key locations like **Desktop, Documents, Downloads, Applications,** and **iCloud Drive.**

- **Main area on the right:** Displays the contents of whatever folder you select.

**To Find a File Quickly:**

1. Open Finder.

2. Use the **Search bar** in the top-right corner.

3. Type a word from the file name, or even a word inside the document.

4. Finder will show results that match.

You can double-click any result to open it.

   **Senior-Friendly Tip:** Don't worry about memorizing file paths. Use the search feature whenever something is "lost." It works just like Google — type what you remember, and your Mac will do the rest.

## How to Use External Drives and USB Sticks

External drives and USB sticks are handy when you want to **back up files**, **transfer**

**documents**, or **share photos** with someone who doesn't use email.

## Plugging It In:

- Insert the USB stick or external drive into your MacBook's port.

- If your Mac has only USB-C ports, you may need a small adapter.

Once connected:

- A new **icon** will appear on your Desktop.

- You'll also see the drive listed in **Finder** under *Locations*.

## Copying Files to the Drive:

1. Open **Finder** and locate the file you want to copy.

2. Click and **drag it** to the USB drive's icon.

3. The file will copy automatically.

**Ejecting Safely:**

Before removing the drive:

- Right-click the drive's icon and select **Eject.**

- Or drag the icon to the Trash (it will change to an eject symbol).

- Once it disappears from the screen, you can safely unplug it.

💡 **Why Eject First?** It prevents your files from being damaged or lost during removal.

## Quick Recap

☑ You learned how to create and save files

☑ You organized your work into folders

☑ You used Finder to locate documents

☑ You safely used USB drives and external storage

Managing your files might seem small, but it brings **a sense of order, control, and peace of mind** — especially when your personal letters, important documents, and precious memories are all right where you can find them.

# Chapter 9: Photos, Music, and Entertainment

Your MacBook is more than just a tool for messages and files — it's a window into your favorite moments and stories. Whether you want to **look through old family photos, listen to your favorite songs,** or **watch a movie on a quiet evening**, your Mac makes it easy and enjoyable.

## Viewing and Organizing Photos

The **Photos app** is where all your pictures live — including those taken on your iPhone (if connected to iCloud) or imported from a USB stick or camera.

**To Open the Photos App:**

- Click the **Photos icon** (a colorful flower) in the Dock or Launchpad.

**Viewing Your Pictures:**

- You'll see **Library**, **Albums**, and **Favorites** on the left.

- Click **Library** to see all your pictures in the order they were taken.

- Double-click any photo to view it larger.

**Organizing Photos into Albums:**

1. In the Photos app, click **File > New Album**.

2. Name your album (e.g., *Family Trip 2023*).

3. Select the photos you want to add.

4. Drag them into your new album.

You can create albums for birthdays, vacations, grandkids — whatever brings you joy.

**Importing Photos from a USB Stick:**

1. Plug in the USB.

2. Open **Photos**.

3. Click **File > Import**, then choose the photos from your USB drive.

4. Click **Review for Import** and then **Import All** (or select the ones you want).

   **Tip:** Mark your favorite pictures with a heart icon — they'll be added to your **Favorites** album automatically.

## Editing and Sharing Memories

You don't need to be a photographer to make your photos look better. The **Edit feature** in the Photos app lets you do simple fixes in a few clicks.

**To Edit a Photo:**

1. Open any photo.

2. Click the **Edit** button (top-right corner).

3. Try these simple tools:

   ○ **Auto** – Let your Mac adjust brightness and contrast automatically.

   ○ **Crop** – Trim out parts of the image.

   ○ **Rotate** – Fix sideways photos.

○ **Filters** – Add fun effects.

When you're happy, click **Done**.

**To Share a Photo:**

1. Select the photo.

2. Click the **Share button** (a square with an upward arrow).

3. Choose how to send it — by **Mail**, **Messages**, or **AirDrop** (for Apple-to-Apple sharing).

## Using Apple Music, Podcasts, and YouTube

Your Mac can play all kinds of audio entertainment — from your favorite oldies to podcasts and radio shows that feel like good company.

**Apple Music (Built-In):**

- Click the **Music app** (a music note icon).

- You can listen to free radio stations or, if you subscribe, access a large library of songs.

- To play a song or album, click **Browse** or use the search bar.

**Bonus Tip:** If you don't want a subscription, you can still enjoy the **Radio tab** inside the Music app — free to use.

**Podcasts (Spoken Audio Shows):**

- Open the **Podcasts app** (purple icon with sound waves).

- Browse by topics — like history, faith, hobbies, or news.

- Click **Follow** to keep up with new episodes automatically.

## YouTube (Through Safari):

1. Open **Safari** and go to www.youtube.com.

2. Use the search bar to look for music videos, shows, or any topic of interest.

3. Click to play. It's that simple.

💡 **Seniors love this:** Type in keywords like "relaxing music," "church sermons," or "classic comedy shows" — and enjoy an endless library of free content.

## Watching TV and Movies on Apple TV

The **Apple TV app** lets you rent or stream movies and shows — both free and paid. You don't need a separate Apple TV device to use it on your MacBook.

## To Open Apple TV:

- Click the **TV icon** in your Dock or Launchpad.

## Inside the App:

- Browse **Watch Now**, **Movies**, and **TV Shows**.

- Some content is free; others may require a rental fee or subscription.

## To Watch Something:

- Click a title, then choose **Play**, **Rent**, or **Subscribe** (depending on availability).

- Sit back and enjoy — full-screen mode makes it feel like your own home theater.

**Extra Tip:** Use **headphones** for better sound or quiet listening late at night.

## Quick Recap

☑ You opened and organized photos in the Photos app

☑ You made basic photo edits and shared pictures easily

☑ You listened to music, podcasts, and browsed YouTube

☑ You watched movies and TV shows using the **Apple TV app**

Whether you're relaxing, reminiscing, or discovering something new, your MacBook opens up a world of entertainment — no cable, no CDs, no fuss. Just click, enjoy, and smile.

# Chapter 10: Staying Safe and Secure

Using a MacBook should feel safe and stress-free — and the good news is, Apple builds its computers with **security in mind**. But just like locking your front door, there are a few simple habits and settings that can help keep your digital life private, secure, and worry-free.

In this chapter, you'll learn how to **create strong passwords, use Touch ID, manage security settings**, and understand basic privacy tips to stay protected online.

## Creating Strong Passwords

Your password is the **first line of defense** in keeping your MacBook and online accounts safe. A strong password is:

- Not easy to guess

- At least 8 characters long

- A mix of letters, numbers, and symbols

How to Change or Set Your Mac Password:

1. Click the **Apple logo** (top-left corner).

2. Go to **System Settings** > **Users & Groups.**

3. Click your account name, then choose **Change Password.**

Make it something **memorable to you** but hard for others to guess. Avoid using names, birthdays, or simple words like "password."

**Tip for Seniors:** If you have trouble remembering passwords, use a **notebook** stored safely at home, or consider a trusted password manager like 1Password or Apple's built-in Keychain.

## Setting Up Touch ID or Password Protection

If your Mac has a **Touch ID button** (usually on newer models), you can use your fingerprint instead of typing your password every time.

**To Set Up Touch ID:**

1. Go to **System Settings** > **Touch ID & Password.**

2. Click **Add Fingerprint**, then place your finger on the Touch ID sensor (usually the top-right key).

3. Follow the on-screen instructions.

Touch ID can be used to:

- Unlock your Mac

- Authorize App Store purchases

- Fill in passwords automatically

If your Mac doesn't have Touch ID, don't worry — a strong password is just as secure.

## Managing Security Settings and Scam Alerts

Apple includes built-in security tools to help keep your Mac safe, but you can add extra layers of protection with just a few clicks.

Turn On Your Firewall:

1. Go to **System Settings** > **Network** > **Firewall**.

2. Toggle it **On** to block unwanted incoming connections.

Enable Automatic Updates:

90

Software updates include important security fixes.

To turn on automatic updates:

1. Go to **System Settings** > **General** > **Software Update.**

2. Make sure **Automatic Updates** is turned on.

This way, your Mac stays up to date and protected — without you needing to do anything else.

## Be Cautious of Scam Pop-Ups and Fake Warnings:

Sometimes, while browsing online, you may see messages that say things like:

- *"Your Mac is infected!"*

- *"Call this number to fix a problem."*

- *"Click here to speed up your computer."*

These are almost always **scams**. **Do not click, call, or download anything** from these pop-ups.

What to do instead:

- Close the browser tab immediately.

- If something won't close, press **Command + Q** to quit the app.

- Restart your Mac and run **System Settings > General > Software Update** just to be safe.

**Friendly Reminder:** Apple will **never** call you or ask for remote access to your computer.

# Using Time Machine to Back Up Your Mac

Backing up your files ensures that you **never lose important documents, photos, or emails**, even if something goes wrong with your Mac.

Apple's backup tool is called **Time Machine** — and once it's set up, it does everything automatically.

**To Use Time Machine:**

1. Plug in an external hard drive (ask for help picking one if needed).

2. Go to **System Settings > Time Machine**.

3. Select the drive and click **Use as Backup Disk**.

Time Machine will now back up your files regularly — no extra work needed.

## Quick Recap

☑ You created a strong Mac password

☑ You set up **Touch ID** (if available)

☑ You enabled key **security settings** and automatic updates

☑ You learned how to avoid online scams and pop-ups

☑ You started protecting your files with **Time Machine backups**

A secure MacBook is a peaceful MacBook — and now that you've got these safety basics covered, you can explore the digital world with confidence and peace of mind.

# Chapter 11: Essential Apps for Everyday Life

Your MacBook is more than just a computer — it's a personal assistant that can help you stay organized, remember important dates, get directions, check the weather, and more. And the best part? Many of these tools come already installed, ready to use.

In this chapter, we'll explore some of the most useful apps for daily living — and show you how to get the most from them with just a few clicks.

## Calendar, Notes, and Reminders

These three apps are great for keeping your life organized — whether you want to remember a doctor's appointment, jot down a recipe, or create a daily to-do list.

## Calendar

The **Calendar app** helps you keep track of birthdays, appointments, holidays, and events.

To open it:

- Click the **Calendar icon** (a red-and-white page) in the Dock.

To add an event:

1. Click the "+" button in the top-left.

2. Enter the event name (e.g., "Lunch with Mary").

3. Choose the **date and time.**

4. Click **Add.**

**Tip:** You can set reminders for upcoming events so your Mac notifies you in advance.

## Notes

The **Notes app** is perfect for writing anything — grocery lists, passwords, gift ideas, or reflections.

To open it:

- Click the **Notes icon** (a yellow-and-white notepad) in the Dock.

To create a note:

1. Click the **New Note** button (a square with a pencil).

2. Start typing. Notes save automatically.

You can also **add checklists**, **insert photos**, or **organize notes into folders**.

Reminders

If you need help remembering tasks, the **Reminders app** is your digital to-do list.

To open it:

- Click the **Reminders icon** (a white list with colored dots).

To create a reminder:

1. Click **New Reminder**.

2. Type your task (e.g., "Take medicine at 8 AM").

3. Add a time or date for a notification.

**Senior-Friendly Tip:** Use Reminders for medications, bill payments, or even "Call grandkids every Sunday."

## Using Maps and Weather

These two apps help you **plan your day**, whether you're going out or just curious about what's happening outside.

**Maps**

The **Maps app** helps you get directions and view places around the world.

To open it:

- Click the **Maps icon** (a blue map symbol).

To find directions:

1. Type the address or name of the place in the search bar.

2. Click **Directions**.

3. Enter your starting point (your address is often added automatically).

4. Choose **Driving**, **Walking**, or **Transit**.

5. Your route will appear with step-by-step directions.

Even if you don't drive, Maps is great for checking distances, finding restaurants, or locating landmarks.

## Weather

The **Weather app** tells you the current conditions and forecast.

To open it:

- Open **Safari**, then go to www.weather.com,

- Or, you can **ask Siri** by saying: *"What's the weather today?"*

You'll see:

- Temperature

- Wind and humidity

- 7-day forecast

**Bonus Tip:** You can add multiple cities (like where your children live) to check their weather too!

## The App Store: How to Download Useful Apps

The **App Store** is where you can find more apps — many are free and designed to make life easier, more fun, or more productive.

To open it:

- Click the **App Store icon** (a white "A" on a blue background).

To download an app:

1. Use the **Search bar** to look for apps like:

   o "Zoom" for video calls

   o "Bible" for daily reading

   o "Solitaire" for games

2. Click the **Get** button (or the price, if it's a paid app).

3. Enter your **Apple ID password or use Touch** ID to confirm.

4. The app will install and appear in your **Launchpad or Dock.**

 **Friendly Suggestion:** Start with one or two simple apps that match your interests — there's no rush to explore them all.

## Quick Recap

☑ You used **Calendar, Notes, and Reminders** to stay organized

☑ You explored **Maps** for directions and **Weather** to plan your day

☑ You learned how to **find and download helpful apps** from the App Store

With just a few basic apps, your MacBook becomes your personal planner, journal, assistant, and daily helper — right at your fingertips.

# Chapter 12:
# Troubleshooting and Tips

Even with a user-friendly device like a MacBook, things don't always go perfectly — and that's okay. Whether a button doesn't respond, a file goes missing, or something just feels "off," this chapter is here to help you **solve common problems quickly and calmly.**

Remember: you can't "break" your MacBook by accident. Most issues have easy fixes, and you're not alone. Let's walk through some of the most helpful tips and tricks.

---

## Fixing Common Problems Step-by-Step

Problem 1: "My screen is frozen."

- **Solution:** Hold down the **Power button** until the screen goes black.

- Wait 10 seconds, then press the button again to restart.

**Tip:** This is called a "force restart." It's safe to do when your Mac isn't responding.

---

### Problem 2: "An app won't close."

- Click the **Apple logo** (top-left), then select **Force Quit.**

- Choose the app that's not responding and click **Force Quit.**

This won't damage your computer — it's like closing a stuck door gently.

---

### Problem 3: "I can't find a file I saved."

- Open **Finder** (smiley face icon).

- Click the **Search bar** (top-right corner) and type part of the file name or a word you remember from inside it.

- If you still can't find it, check **Downloads**, **Documents**, or **Desktop** in the Finder sidebar.

---

## Problem 4: "I have no sound."

- Make sure your **volume is up** (use the speaker keys at the top of your keyboard).

- Go to **System Settings > Sound** and check if the correct speaker is selected.

- If using headphones, make sure they're plugged in properly or connected via Bluetooth.

## Problem 5: "My Wi-Fi isn't working."

- Click the **Wi-Fi icon** at the top of the screen.

- Turn Wi-Fi **Off**, then turn it **Back On**.

- If needed, restart your Mac and reconnect to your home network.

**Senior Tip:** If a problem persists, restarting your Mac often fixes it. Don't be afraid to try a reboot first.

## When to Restart or Update

Like any machine, your Mac sometimes needs a refresh.

107

**When to Restart:**

- Apps are running slowly

- You notice glitches or lag

- The system feels "stuck"

Click the **Apple logo** > **Restart**. Wait for it to shut down and start back up — this clears out small memory issues.

**When to Update:**

- You're asked to install updates

- You want the latest features or security fixes

To check for updates:

1. Click the **Apple logo** > **System Settings**.

2. Choose **Software Update**.

3. If an update is available, click **Update Now.**

Apple updates are safe and usually take just a few minutes.

## Where to Get Help (Apple Support and Forums)

You never have to face a problem alone — there's plenty of help available.

### 1. Apple Support Website:

Go to support.apple.com

Type your question (e.g., "how to print a photo") and browse helpful articles.

### 2. Apple Support App:

Download the free **Apple Support** app from the App Store. It offers live chat, tutorials, and scheduling help.

### 3. In-Person Help:

Visit an **Apple Store** and speak with a **Genius Bar technician** — appointments are free.

**Tip:** Bring your MacBook and your Apple ID details if you go in person.

## Resetting or Shutting Down Properly

**To Shut Down:**

1. Click the **Apple logo**.

2. Select **Shut Down**.

3. Wait for the screen to go black before closing the lid.

**To Reset (if your Mac is misbehaving):**

- Use **Restart** from the same menu. This won't delete any files — it simply refreshes the system.

**Important:** Only do a full reset (factory reset) if advised by Apple Support or you're giving your Mac away.

## Quick Recap

☑ You learned how to fix common problems like freezing, no sound, or missing files

☑ You understood when and how to **restart or update** your Mac

☑ You discovered where to **get trustworthy help**, both online and in person

☑ You practiced safe shutdowns and resets

Technology might act up sometimes, but now **you know exactly what to do — calmly, clearly, and confidently.** You've come a long way, and you've got the tools to keep going strong.

# BONUS SECTION: Quick Reference & Handy Guides

This bonus section is your **MacBook cheat sheet** — perfect for quick reminders, simple fixes, and day-to-day help without having to search through the entire book.

## MacBook Keyboard Shortcuts (Senior-Friendly List)

These simple keyboard shortcuts can save you time:

- Command (⌘) + C = Copy

- Command (⌘) + V = Paste

- Command (⌘) + Z = Undo

- Command (⌘) + Q = Quit App

- Command (⌘) + P = Print

- **Command (⌘) + Spacebar** = Open Spotlight Search

- **Command (⌘) + Tab** = Switch between open apps

- **Command (⌘) + Shift + 3** = Take a screenshot of your screen

Tip: Don't worry if you forget these. You can always do tasks manually — shortcuts are just optional time-savers.

## Internet Safety Checklist

Before clicking or typing on any website:

☑ Is the website address correct? (Watch out for strange spellings.)

☑ Does it begin with "**https**"? (The **s** means secure.)

☑ Are you avoiding pop-ups that say "Your

Mac is infected"?

☑ Never share bank info, passwords, or personal details unless it's a trusted site.

☑ If unsure — close the page. You can always ask someone or check with Apple.

## Daily Mac Maintenance Tips

Keeping your Mac in good shape is easy when done a little at a time:

- ✓ **Close apps you're not using** to keep things running smoothly

- ✓ **Restart your Mac once a week** — clears out small errors

- ✓ **Back up using Time Machine weekly** (if set up)

- ✓ **Clean your keyboard and screen gently** with a soft cloth

- ✔ Delete old files you no longer need — keeps your Mac tidy and fast

## Glossary: Common Tech Terms Made Simple

**App** – A program that lets you do something, like email or photos

**Dock** – The row of icons at the bottom of your screen

**Finder** – A tool to browse and open your files and folders

**iCloud** – Apple's online storage for photos, files, and backups

**Touch ID** – A fingerprint button to unlock your Mac

**Menu Bar** – The top strip of your screen with system options

**Wi-Fi** – Wireless connection to the internet

**Bluetooth** – Wireless connection for

headphones, speakers, or keyboards

**System Settings** – Where you adjust your Mac's setup (also called Preferences)

**Safari** – Apple's internet browser

**Desktop** – The "home" screen where your folders or files can be placed

## End-of-Chapter Checklist: Have You...?

Learned how to turn on, set up, and personalize your MacBook

Connected to Wi-Fi, used Safari, and sent your first email

Made a FaceTime or video call to a friend or family member

Organized files and photos into folders or albums

Explored music, podcasts, or movies

Learned how to fix simple issues and get

help when needed

▨ Gained the confidence to explore apps that suit your life and interests

If you've checked most of these, you've come a long way — and your MacBook is now a helpful part of your everyday routine.

# Final Words: A Note from the Author

Dear Reader,

If you've made it to this final page, I want you to pause for a moment — and be proud.

You didn't just open a book. You opened the door to learning something new, something that may have once felt intimidating or even out of reach. And you did it with patience, curiosity, and courage.

Whether you started this journey to reconnect with loved ones, explore the internet, organize your memories, or simply feel more independent in a digital world — I hope this guide has helped you feel more at home with your MacBook, and more confident in your abilities.

Remember, learning doesn't stop here. You can go back to any chapter when you need a refresher. You can try new apps, explore new tools, or simply enjoy your favorite features with ease.

And if things go wrong sometimes? That's okay. Everyone — yes, everyone — has moments of confusion with technology. But now you know how to handle those moments, calmly and clearly.

Your MacBook is powerful, but so are you. So go ahead — explore, create, connect, and enjoy every moment.

With all my encouragement,
[ALBERT F. JOHNSON]

www.ingramcontent.com/pod-product-compliance
Lightning Source LLC
LaVergne TN
LVHW051702050326
832903LV00032B/3962